DEVELOPING COMPREHENSION

Green Book

Alan Lynskey

Margaret Stillie

Basil Blackwell

Contents

Introduction

Developing Comprehension is an attempt to clarify and to develop the many skills involved in the real comprehension of language.

The Barrett taxomony, on which the series is based, presents five main categories of comprehension.

1 Literal comprehension: answering questions by direct reference to the text. These answers are usually explicitly stated in the passage.

2 Reorganisational comprehension: classifying, collecting and organising information explicitly stated in the passage. The information may be collected from more than one source.

3 Inferential comprehension: detecting information implied in a passage. This demands thinking and deduction beyond what appears in the passage.

4 Evaluative comprehension: interpreting and evaluating the writer's assumptions or intentions, often by comparison with the reader's own experiences or opinions.

5 Appreciative comprehension: responding to a passage with enjoyment, and with an awareness of its language usage and emotion.

Obviously these skills are not clear cut and separate. There is a considerable overlap between categories. Certainly the higher-level skills — the ability to appreciate and evaluate written material — require the child to exercise literal and re-organisational skills in order to reach decisions.

Techniques

Developing Comprehension uses a variety of techniques to develop reading skills:

Prediction

Predictions are vital to the reader's active involvement in what he or she is reading. In the exercises we ask "What do you think happens next?" In the classroom children should be asked to discuss their predictions and the evidence which supports them. Teachers can give more practice in prediction by breaking a passage into sections and asking "Where do you think this is happening?" "What will so-and-so do next?" "What will happen then?". When the next section is read, the children can evaluate and revise their predictions in the light of what they have learnt.

Cloze texts

These are passages with words omitted, which children are asked to supply. Often there is no right or wrong answer. The child is asked to supply the best word he or she can think of which contributes to the meaning and the feeling of the pasage. If the chosen word can be justified, then it can be judged as right. Sometimes the missing word will be determined by the structure of the sentence, and there will be little argument. But in every case, discussion of alternatives and reasons for choices is vital to the learning process.

Sequencing and ordering

The child is asked to place events in order or sequence. Technically, he or she will need to be able to pick up indicator clues (next, but, etc.) which relate one paragraph to another, and to comprehend the underlying pattern of a passage — to understand across whole paragraphs the development of events. These passages are especially valuable when used in small group discussion. Some whole-class oral work will complete the lesson.

Evaluation

The teacher needs to have clear purposes of evaluation. *Developing Comprehension* is designed to evaluate and improve children's ability to read and fully comprehend. Answers, therefore, should be evaluated initially by the way they display the child's understanding and appreciation of what he or she has read. Classroom discussions should begin with meaning, before looking at how to record that meaning in written English.

The work produced, written or oral, indicates to the teacher the strengths and weaknesses of each child. Programmes of work can be developed to cater for the weaknesses of individuals or groups of children.

The evaluation of responses to cloze texts and prediction and sequencing exercises will be oral as comparisons are made and reasons put forward as to why one choice is better or worse than another. Discussion sessions are crucial in helping children to see what they have missed in their reading, and they encourage purposeful re-reading, which is a vital higher-level skill.

Marking and assessment

The responses or answers a child makes are a starting point for teaching, not a final assessment. Even a totally inappropriate answer will provide a basis on which to work.

The level of difficulty of a passage in relation to a child's reading level must be taken into account in any assessment. No child can be expected to make an evaluation or appreciation of a passage he or she can read only with difficulty. But teacher expectation is a significant factor in pupils' attainment and should not be pitched too low.

We have chosen passages of high literary merit, including the best writers of contemporary children's fiction. We hope that children will be encouraged to read more of the work of the writers they have enjoyed.

ALAN LYNSKEY
MARGARET STILLIE

The battle

The history teacher is telling the class all about William the Conqueror and the time when he marched on an English city because they wouldn't pay his taxes. Then the teacher takes them to the park to act the battle.

"Please can we act the battle?"

"Yes. Get your armour. Kneeshaw, pick a side. And let me see, yes, Tyke, you pick a side . . ."

"That's not fair . . ."

5   "Of course it is."

We chose our sides, Kneeshaw and me.

"We'll toss for who are to be the English and who the Normans."

I felt lucky. I was sure we'd win the toss and we did.
10 Kneebags pulled his ugly mug at me. I didn't care. We climbed the hill and looked down on the others, the enemy. William the Conqueror Kneeshaw and his mob. Pitthead, beside me, made a rude gesture of defiance, as Sir called it, and we rushed down shouting into battle. The sun was hot on the red
15 walls. A great deal of blood must have flowed there. I ran for Kneeshaw and banged his shield with my sword.

"Fight for Kneeshaw!"

"No, fight for Tiler, and England," I called.

I banged him on the helmet and he fell backwards over a
20 tree root, and sat down hurriedly. I fell on him and our armour got tangled up. I pulled his hair. His helmet fell off. The armour slid off us. Sir blew the whistle and the battle was over.

We lay stretched out under the trees. Sir said something to Patsy Drew and another girl and they went off. When they
25 came back they'd got ice lollies for everyone. We lay and licked them under the shade of the trees growing by the old,

red walls. Going back, we walked to the rhythm of:

> Julius Caesar,
> The Roman geezer,
> Squashed his wife with a lemon squeezer.

It wasn't a bad sort of day.

The Turbulent Term of Tyke Tiler
Gene Kemp

1 Who is telling the story?
2 Which two children picked sides?
3 How did they decide who were to be English and who were Normans?
4 What is Kneeshaw's nickname?
5 What is a "rude gesture of defiance"?
6 Describe the fight between Kneeshaw and Tiler.
7 Can you think of any reason why Tyke says "That's not fair" when the teacher chooses who picks sides?
8 Who do you think won the battle?
9 How do you know that Tyke had enjoyed the outing?
10 Do you think Tyke and his class learned anything from this outing? Does acting out battles help you to understand how people of long ago felt and lived?
11 How did the children feel walking back to school, keeping time to the tune? Write about a time you went out with your class and finished up singing.

In hospital

The boy in this story, nicknamed Mouse, remembers the time he had to go into hospital to have his tonsils out.

It is an American story: "flashlight" is the American word for a torch.

He recalled the time he had had his tonsils out, how lightly his mother had treated that. She had said, "Look, it's just your tonsils — those little things on the back of your throat. Don't make a big deal out of it."

5   But it had been a big deal to him. He could still remember the feeling of being in the hospital, of lying in a strange bed. The only reason he had been able to survive that night at all was because, at the last minute, his father had gone down to the car and brought up his flashlight. It was a big, heavy metal
10   flashlight that his father kept in the car in case of an emergency on the road. His father had brought the flashlight out from under his jacket and quickly poked it under the covers. "There, now you'll be all right."

    The flashlight had made Mouse feel better. The cold metal
15   against his leg had calmed him. And when all the other children had gone to sleep and he alone had lain there awake, he had turned on the flashlight and shone it on the faces of the other children in the ward. He could remember right now the way their faces had looked in the pale circle of light. He
20   thought that if he saw one of those children on the street right now today, he would recognise him and go up and say, "Hey, weren't you in the hospital one time?"

The Eighteenth Emergency
Betsy Byars

1 Why was Mouse in hospital?
2 How did the flashlight make him feel better?
3 Where did Mouse's father usually keep the torch? Why?
4 Where did his father hide the torch for Mouse?
5 How did his mother describe Mouse's tonsils?
6 How do you think Mouse felt in hospital at first?
7 Did Mouse's mother understand how he felt at first? Why did she say what she did?
8 Why do you think his father poked the flashlight *quickly* under the covers?
9 Do you think his father knew how Mouse felt? Does this tell you anything about Mouse and his father?
10 Talk or write about any time you have been in hospital or stayed away from home on your own. What happened? What did it feel like at first?

April Fools' Day

These children live in another country. Just like in this country everybody, including your teacher, has to be careful on the first of April.

On the first of April we had fun fooling Miss Johnson, our teacher, as you should on April Fools' Day.

Usually we start school at eight o'clock in the morning, but the day before April the first we all decided to go to school at
5 six the next morning. Just before Miss Johnson locked the door of the schoolroom after our last lesson, Lars ran in and moved the hands of the clock in the schoolroom two hours ahead.

The next day we all got to school at six o'clock, but the clock
10 on the wall in the schoolroom said eight.

We made all the noise we could outside the schoolroom door so that Miss Johnson would hear us. When she didn't come, Lars ran up the second floor and knocked on her door. She lives over the school.

15 "Who is it?" asked Miss Johnson, in a sleepy voice.

"It's Lars," he said. "Aren't we going to have any school today?"

"My goodness, I've overslept," said Miss Johnson. "I'll be down in a minute."

20 Miss Johnson has a clock up in her room too, of course, but she was in such a hurry that she forgot to look at it.

The clock in the schoolroom said twenty minutes past eight when Miss Johnson came down to let us in.

"I can't understand why my alarm clock didn't ring and
25 wake me up," she said.

My, how hard it was for us to keep from laughing when she said that!

We had arithmetic for the first lesson. And just as we were reciting the multiplication table, we heard the alarm clock ringing up in Miss Johonson's room upstairs.

It was really seven o'clock then. But the clock in the schoolroom showed nine.

"What now?" said Miss Johnson.

"April fool! April fool!" we all yelled.

It's only on the first of April that you can say things like that to your teacher.

"Such children!" Miss Johnson said.

All About the Bullerby Children
Astrid Lindgren

1 What time did the children usually start school?
2 Why did the children make a noise outside the schoolroom on April Fools' Day?
3 When did Lars move the clock?
4 Why didn't Miss Johnson notice the time when she got up?
5 When did Miss Johnson realise she had been tricked?
6 Do you think this is a big or small school? Give the reasons for your answer.
7 In what ways is this school different from most in England?
8 Do you think the teacher was cross with the children or did she think it was a good trick?
9 How long did it take Miss Johnson to get to the schoolroom?
10 Is there any way Miss Johnson could have got her own back on the children?
11 Write about any tricks you have played on people on April Fools' Day.

Minnow thoughts

A minnow is a very little fish, and he has a very little brain. He never learns to add and subtract, but this small brain teaches him things a minnow needs to know.

5   He needs to know that he should always stay with his own school of minnows. He only feels safe when he is with his school. Drop a stone in the water, and the whole school of minnows quickly swims away. If one minnow swims away from the school and finds himself alone, he begins to swim wildly this way and that. He swims very fast, until he finds his
10   school again.

    Scientists like to find out why animals act the way they do. They found out that one tiny part of the minnow's brain makes him stay with his school. Then the scientists found out how to remove this tiny part of the minnow's brain without hurting the
15   minnow. They took one minnow and removed this special part. Then they put him back in the water with his school.

    The special minnow looked at his friends. Then he flicked his tail and swam off alone. He wasn't afraid at all. This was just what the scientists expected. But what happened next
20   surprised them.

    The whole school of minnows swam after the one special minnow!

Emily Neville

1 What does the word "school" mean when talking of minnows?

2 What is the most important thing a minnow needs to know?

3 What happens when a minnow is separated from its school?

4 In your own words describe what the scientists did to the minnow. Do you think this operation would be difficult to perform? Why?

5 Why did the minnow with part of its brain removed swim off alone?

6 In what way were the scientists surprised?

7 Do you think a school of minnows has a leader or not? Give a reason for your answer.

8 The writer says scientists like to know about animal behaviour. Do you think this is useful to us? Give reasons for your answer.

9 What feeling did the minnow lose after the operation on its brain? Do you think humans have a feeling like that?

10 The passage describes what scientists sometimes do to animals. Do you think animals should be used in this way? Give reasons for your answer.

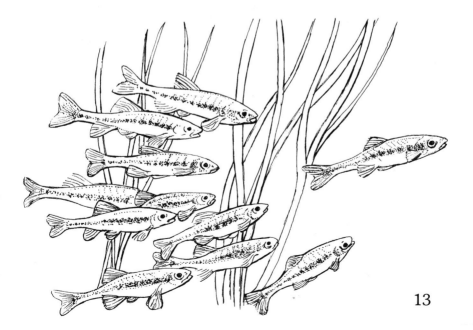

Visiting Victor's house

Andrew and his family move to a new place where many things are different. Andrew makes friends with Victor, who is not like anyone he has met before. His house is different, too.

"I like houses a bit dirty," said Victor. "They smell nice and warm."

Andrew thought that this was rather an odd remark, until he arrived at Victor's house on Friday afternoon. Victor gave
5 Andrew a lift on the back of his bike and they wobbled to a halt outside his gate just before three o'clock.

Victor parked the bicycle and went into the conservatory, making a great deal of noise wiping his feet. Andrew thought it wise to do the same. From the doorway, Victor's house had
10 an unpleasantly shiny look about it and smelt like a dentist's waiting room. He began to see why Victor liked dirty houses.

Victor's mother was in the kitchen. She didn't say hello, she said, "Don't make a mess on the floor, I've just cleaned it."

Victor said, "We've wiped our feet. Mum, this is Andrew
15 Mitchell."

Andrew said, "Good afternoon, Mrs Skelton."

Victor's mother said, "You can't play in the lounge, I've got the vacuum cleaner in there. Mind where you're walking. I've just polished that bit."
20 The kitchen floor was laid with white tiles. There were a few black ones, here and there. Andrew thought that it might have been better the other way round.

"I came third in the mile," said Victor.

"Not in those shoes, I hope," said his mother. "You'd better
25 go on up to your room. I'll call you when tea's ready."

Victor set off across the kitchen, using the black tiles as

stepping stones. Andrew followed him. The black tiles were a long way apart.

Thunder and Lightnings
Jan Mark

1 How did Andrew get to Victor's house?
2 Why couldn't the boys play in the lounge?
3 How did Victor's house first seem to Andrew?
4 What were the first words Victor's mother spoke?
5 What do these words tell you about her?
6 What does her reply to "I came third in the mile" tell you about her?
7 Why do you think Victor made a great deal of noise wiping his feet?
8 Why did Andrew copy everything Victor did?
9 Why did Mrs Skelton send them up to Victor's room?
10 What do you think Andrew's house was like?
11 Why did Andrew think the tiles might have been better the other way round?
12 What sort of house do you like? Do you agree with Victor's first remark? Think of any time you have visited a house for the first time. How did you feel?

The end of winter

Laura and her family lived in a very remote part of America. They had to build their own house, make everything they needed, and grow or hunt all their food. When the snow came, it was a very hard life until the special wind called the Chinook brought warmer weather.

She listened as hard as she could. She uncovered her ear to listen and the cold did not bite her cheek. The dark was warmer. She put out her hand and felt only a coolness. The little sound that she heard was a trickling of waterdrops. The
5 eaves were dripping. Then she knew.

She sprang up in bed and called aloud, "Pa! Pa! The Chinook is blowing!"

"I hear it, Laura," Pa answered from the other room. "Spring has come. Go back to sleep."

10 The Chinook was blowing. Spring had come. The blizzard had given up; it was driven back to the north. Blissfully Laura stretched out in bed; she put both arms on top of the quilts and they were not very cold. She listened to the blowing wind and dripping eaves and she knew that in the other room Pa
15 was lying awake, too, listening and glad. The Chinook, the wind of spring, was blowing. Winter was ended.

In the morning the snow was nearly gone. The frost was melted from the windows, and outdoors the air was soft and warm.

20 Pa was whistling as he came from doing the chores.

"Well girls," he said gaily. "We beat old Winter at last! Here is spring, and none of us lost or starved or frozen! Anyway, not much frozen."

Mary pushed her chair back from the stove. "It is really too
25 warm, so close to the fire," she said.

16

Carrie would hardly leave the window. "I like to see the water run," she explained.

Laura said nothing; she was too happy. She could hardly believe that the winter was gone, that spring had come. When Pa asked her why she was so silent, she answered soberly, "I said it all in the night."

"I should say you did! Waking us all from a sound sleep to tell us the wind was blowing!" Pa teased her. "As if the wind hadn't blown for months!"

"I said the Chinook," Laura reminded him. "That makes all the difference."

The Long Winter
Laura Ingalls Wilder

1 What else is the Chinook called?
2 What did they find had happened in the morning?
3 Why did Carrie stay by the window?
4 Why could Laura not say anything?
5 What sound did Laura hear?
6 Do you think Laura was surprised when she uncovered her ear? What was she expecting?
7 Do you think Pa was cross at being woken up in the night? Why?
8 Do you think it had been a hard winter? Why?
9 Read what Mary says. What does this tell you about the weather the Chinook brought?
10 Is it usual to be silent like Laura was when you are happy? Does this tell you anything about the sort of child Laura was?
11 Write other words you could use instead of

blissfully (line 11)   chores (line 20)
soberly (line 30)   blizzard (line 10)

12 Which words or phrases in the passage tell you that Pa was happy?

Jumping

	LONG JUMP	TRIPLE JUMP
Order of jumping	This is decided by drawing lots.	Lots are drawn.
Number of jumps	Each competitor is allowed three jumps and the best of the three counts.	The longest jump of the three b{ each competitor is the winner.
No jumps	1 It is a "No jump" if the jumper's hands, or any other part of his body, touch the ground outside the pit *nearer* to the board than the mark in the sand. 2 It is a "no jump" if the jumper's feet touch the ground in front of the take-off board.	1 It is a "no jump" if the jumpe hands, or any other part of his body, touch the ground outside pit *nearer* to the board than the mark in the sand. 2 It is a "no jump" if the jumpe feet touch the ground in front o the take-off board.
The tie rule	If two competitors both have the longest jump, the winner is the one who has the longest second jump. Remember each competitor had three jumps. So the second jumps of each are compared and the competitor whose second jump was longest wins.	Each competitor has three jump the third jumps are equal then { competitor with the longest seco jump is the winner.

In athletics there are four jumping events — two horizontal and two vertical. Above are some of the rules for these events. Read them then use the chart to answer the questions.

1 How is the order of jumping in the pole vault decided?
2 How many jumps may each competitor have in each event?
3 Look at the rules for "no jumps". Write down the ones that apply to *both* high jump and pole vault.
4 How can a competitor be knocked out of the pole vault competition?
5 Look up the words "vertical" and "horizontal" in your

H JUMP	POLE VAULT
is drawn by lots.	This is drawn by lots.
ı competitor may have three tries to ˙ each height. If he fails three times he is of the competition.	Three "no jump" at any height means that the competitor drops out.
a failure or "no jump" if in your attempt ɘar the bar you ˙nock the bar so that it falls from its pegs; ˙ake a two-footed take off; ˙uch the ground or landing area under ˙ beyond the bar without first ɘaring the bar.	It is a failure or "no jump" if you 1 knock the bar with your body or the pole so that it falls from the pegs; 2 touch the ground beyond the bar with your body or the pole before clearing the bar; 3 leave the ground to make a vault but fail to clear the bar; 4 Move your lower hand above your upper hand or move your upper hand further up the pole at the moment of making the vault or after leaving the ground.
ɔ competitors tie then the winner is the ⸜who has made the lowest number of ᴣs at the height at which the tie occurs.	If two competitors fail three times at the same height the one with the least number of failures at the lower height wins.
ɑrning to be a Better Athlete	

dictionary. Write down the names of the two "horizontal" jumps.

6 Which of the four jumps do you think would be the hardest to learn? Why?

7 In which jumps could the second best jump decide the winner?

8 In which jump is a two-footed take off banned?

9 Which two events do you think are most alike?

10 How is the pole vault different from the others?

11 The 'Triple Jump' used to be called 'The Hop, Step and Jump'; why do you think the name was changed?

Tilly's puppies

Ben wants a puppy more than anything in the world. His dreams and imagination are full of puppies. Then his Grandpa's dog Tilly has a litter.

They went to see Tilly's puppies. She did not want them to go; but, if they were going, she knew that her duty was to go too, and to go ahead. She went briskly but with a waddle, being incommoded by the swinging heaviness of the milk for
5　her puppies.

The sty had once belonged to some pigs, but was now perfectly clean, with plenty of fresh straw on the concrete floor and a special lamp suspended low from one corner of the roof to give a gentle heat. Beneath this the puppies had all crawled
10　and crowded together, and lay sleeping, a large, thick, sleek blob of multiple puppy-life.

Grandpa and Ben stooped under the corrugated iron roof of the sty and sat down on upturned buckets padded with folded sacking. Tilly had gone in front of them, but now she
15　stood a little to one side and behind, very quietly. "She's not keen on their knowing she's here at all," said Grandpa. "She knows they'll be squeaking and pushing after her milk, once they do know. And they're none of 'em starving."

Grandpa plunged his fingers into the heap of puppies and
20　brought one out at random. He dropped it into Ben's cupped hands. It just filled them — as a full grown Chihuahua might have done, Ben thought. "Chiquitito!" he said softly.

Ben felt perfect happiness. He shifted the puppy into one hand — which it slightly overflowed — in order to be able to
25　stroke it with the back of the forefinger of his other hand. Then he put it down and gently picked up another. The puppies varied in size, but all were sleek-coated and fat.

A Dog so Small
Philippa Pearce

1 Where were the puppies?
2 Where did Ben and Grandpa sit?
3 What was the special lamp for?
4 Why did Tilly go with Ben and his Grandpa?
5 How had the shed been altered since it was a pigsty?
6 Why do you think they put straw on the concrete floor?
7 Why didn't Tilly want her puppies to know she was there?
8 How did Ben feel with the puppy in his hands? Do you think he would make any sound? Would you?
9 "A large, thick, sleek blob of multiple puppy-life." What does this tell you about the puppies and how they were lying? Do you think this is a good description?
10 Write a short, careful description of an animal you like. Try to make your reader like it, too.
11 Use your dictionary to find out what these words in the passage mean.

   stooped (line 12)   random (line 20)   varied (line 27)
   sleek (line 10)   multiple (line 11)
   incommoded (line 4)

Stig's cave

Barney knew that the edge of the chalkpit would crumble away if he got too near. One day it did crumble and he had a terrible shock. He found a shaggy-haired boy who lived in a sort of cave full of his own inventions.

He'd never seen anything like the collection of bits and pieces, odds and ends, bric-a-brac and old brock, that this Stig creature had lying about his den. There were stones and bones, fossils and bottles, skins and tins, stacks of sticks and
5 hanks of string. There were motor-car tyres and hats from old scarecrows, nuts and bolts and bobbles from brass bedsteads. There was a coal scuttle full of dead electric light bulbs and a basin with rusty screws and nails in it. There was a pile of bracken and newspapers that looked as if it were used for a
10 bed. The place looked as if it had never been given a tidy-up.
"I wish I lived here," said Barney.
Stig seemed to understand that Barney was approving of his home and his face lit up. He took on the air of a householder showing a visitor round his property, and began
15 pointing out some of the things he seemed particularly proud of.
First, the plumbing. Where the water dripped through a crack in the roof of the cave he had wedged the mud-guard of a bicycle. The water ran along this, through the tube of a
20 vacuum cleaner, and into a big can with writing on it. By the side of this was a plastic football carefully cut in half, and Stig dipped up some water and offered it to Barney. Barney had swallowed a mouthful before he made out the writing on the can: it said Weedkiller. However, the water only tasted of rust
25 and rubber.
It was dark in the back of the cave. Stig went to the front where the ashes of a fire were smoking faintly, blew on them,

22

picked up a book that lay beside his bed, tore out a page and rolled it up, lit it at the fire, and carried it to a lamp set in a niche in the wall. As it flared up Barney could see it was in fact an old teapot, filled with some kind of oil, and with a bootlace hanging out of it for a wick.

Stig of the Dump
Clive King

1 Write down seven things Barney sees lying about Stig's cave.
2 What was in the coal scuttle?
3 What were the bracken and newspapers probably used for?
4 Why did Stig's face light up (line 13)?
5 How did Stig feel about his cave? In your own words describe his feelings and actions when Barney seemed to like it.
6 Say what each of the following items was used for: the bicycle mud-guard; the book; the teapot; the newspapers; the half-football.
7 Do you think Stig had lived there for a long time? Give as many reasons as you can for your answer.
8 Where do you think Stig did his cooking?
9 Why do you think the fire was at the front of the cave?
10 Draw a picture of Stig's plumbing. By your picture write what the equipment is and what job it does.
11 Why would Barney wish he lived in a place like Stig's?
12 What do you think Barney's house was like? How would it compare with Stig's?

The water cycle

The passages below are about the water cycle. The first two paragraphs are given in the correct order. The sentences below tell the same story but are in a mixed-up order. Read paragraphs one and two carefully. They will help you put the mixed-up sentences which follow in the correct order.

When you have found the correct order write out the sentences as they should be written.

There is always water vapour in the air. When air is cooled the vapour condenses into millions of tiny particles of water which come together to form clouds. If the condensation continues, the water particles get too big and heavy for the air to hold them up and so they fall to the earth, mainly as rain.

The water vapour in the air reaches the earth in many forms: as rain, hail, snow, sleet and even dew, hoar and frost. Weathermen have one name to cover them all — precipitation.

A It rises higher and higher and gets colder and then it condenses into clouds.

B The clouds then become even colder.

C Most of the water that falls on the earth is taken back by rivers to the oceans, seas and lakes again.

D Water evaporates into the air from seas, lakes, ponds, rivers and all wet surfaces.

E These are blown along by the wind until they meet colder air or until they meet obstacles such as mountains, which cause them to rise.

F The whole sequence is called the water cycle.

G This causes the vapour to condense into water which falls as rain.

H Three things take place in the process: evaporation, condensation and precipitation.

The Young Geographer

The greengrocer's stall

You are going to draw a picture of a greengrocer's stall. You can label any items you like.

1   Draw a rectangle as large as your paper allows.

2   From the middle of the top line, draw one line to the bottom left-hand corner and one line to the bottom right-hand corner. You should now have three triangles. Write "Fruit" on the middle triangle, "Flowers" on the left-hand triangle, and "Vegetables" on the right-hand triangle.

3   In the bottom corner of the flower section are six red plants with small green leaves. At the top are bunches of mixed flowers and in between are yellow flowers standing in tall jars.

4   At the bottom of the centre triangle the greengrocer put three types of fruit — bananas nearest to the red plants, black grapes in the opposite corner and pears in between. At the top he put six rows of oranges. Each row has one more orange than the row above it. In the middle of the fruit section the greengrocer placed some apples: red ones above the bananas, green ones above the pears and golden ones above the grapes.

5   Potatoes are at the top of the vegetable triangle. Below them are four rows of onions. At the bottom are five large cauliflowers with carrots above them. In between the carrots and onions are six cabbages.

The Iron Man captured

The Iron Man has been eating the machinery and metal on the farms. So the farmers dug a huge pit to trap him. But the Iron Man never came near the pit. Then the boy Hogarth had an idea.

In his pocket, among other things, he had a long nail and a knife. He took these out. Did he dare? His idea frightened him. In the silent dusk, he tapped the nail and the knife blade together.

5 Clink, clink, clink!

At the sound of the metal, the Iron Man's hands became still. After a few seconds, he slowly turned his head and the headlamp eyes shone towards Hogarth.

Again, Clink, clink, clink! went the nail on the knife.

10 Slowly, the Iron Man took three strides towards Hogarth, and again stopped. It was now quite dark. The headlamps shone red. Hogarth pressed close to the tree trunk. Between him and the Iron Man lay the wide lid of the trap.

Clink, clink, clink! again he tapped the nail on the knife.

15 And now the Iron Man was coming. Hogarth could feel the earth shaking under the weight of his footsteps. Was it too late to run? Hogarth stared at the Iron Man, looming, searching towards him for the taste of the metal that had made that inviting sound.

20 Clink, clink, clink! went the nail on the knife. And CRASSSHHH!

The Iron Man vanished.

He was in the pit. The Iron Man had fallen into the pit. Hogarth went close. The earth was shaking as the Iron Man

25 struggled underground. Hogarth peered over the torn edge of the great pit. Far below, two deep red headlamps glared up at him from the pitch blackness. He could hear the Iron Man's

insides grinding down there and it sounded like a big lorry grinding its gears on a steep hill. Hogarth set off. He ran, he ran, home — home with the great news. And as he passed the cottages on the way, and as he turned down the lane towards his father's farm, he was shouting "The Iron Man's in the trap!" and "We've caught the Iron Giant!"

The Iron Man
Ted Hughes

1 What attracted the Iron Man's attention?
2 What lay between Hogarth and the Iron Man?
3 How did Hogarth know the Iron Man was coming?
4 What happened at the first sound of the metal?
5 Read the passage carefully, then, in your own words, tell how the Iron Man was finally trapped.
6 The passage tells us quite a lot about the Iron Man. Write what you think he looked like.
7 Why do you think Hogarth "pressed close to the tree trunk"?
8 Why do you think Hogarth *ran* home with the news?
9 How do you think the farmers felt when they saw the Iron Man in the pit?
10 How do you think Hogarth felt when the Iron Man was trapped?
11 Write out these sentences completely using the words from the brackets which you think make the best sense. Give the reasons for your choices.

a) The Iron Man followed the noises because [he was anxious/he was frightened/he was hungry].

b) Hogarth thought about running away because [he felt sorry for the Iron Man/he was ashamed of what he was doing/he was frightened].

The fox and the geese

Read this passage. When you have read it, make a list of the numbers in your book and write the best word you think should go in each blank space.

The fox was hungry. He was always hungry. Never could he catch enough to satisfy his . . .1. . . appetite.

One day he . . .2. . . out of the wood where he had been trying, in vain, to find a nice plump rabbit for his dinner, when there, right in front of his eyes, what should he see but a row of seven . . .3. . . geese sitting in the middle of a green field.

"What luck!" said the fox to himself. "I will eat them all. What a . . .4. . . they will make!"

He stalked boldly up to the seven fat geese, and said aloud, "Good morning, my dears! What a fine dinner you will make. It's no good looking . . .5. . ., for you can't get away. I shall eat you one by one, beginning with the fattest."

Then he grinned a . . .6. . . grin, showing all his . . .7. . . and licked his lips with his . . .8. . . red tongue.

The geese were very . . .9. . . and began to look the picture of misery. They had no idea what to say to the . . .10. . . fox. But at last one of them spoke up boldly and said, "Mr Fox, we know we cannot get away. You can run much . . .11. . . than we can. It is clear that we must . . .12. . . to make your dinner. But . . .13. . . Mr Fox, will you grant us one favour?"

A Story With No End
James Reeves

Talk about the words you and your friends have chosen, and decide which ones fit in best. Make sure you always have a reason for your choice.

The Queen's magician

Now do the same with this passage.

The Queen's magician lived at the top of the old tower in the palace grounds. Here, like a spider in a hole, he spent his days . . .*1*. . . spells, mixing potions, stirring his brews over a strange . . .*2*. . . of green and blue flames. The damp stone walls were hung . . .*3*. . . black draperies, and the dried skins of bat and bird, . . .*4*. . . and salamander. Bundles of herbs filled the dusty shelves.

He . . .*5*. . . a tattered robe ornamented with stars and crescents out of which his . . .*6*. . . skinny arms and pointed fingers poked like the twigs of a dead . . .*7*. . . and his head under a velvet skull cap, was . . .*8*. . . yellow as old ivory and as smooth as an egg. His . . .*9*. . . was nothing but a high, bony forehead, a sharp beaky nose and a sharper chin, with burning dark . . .*10*. . . glowing like lamps within his skull. For more years than he could . . .*11*. . . he had been trying to turn base metals into gold, but though the Queen loved . . .*12*. . . more than anything else in the world, all her magic and his arts could . . .*13*. . . produce it.

The Golden Bird
Edith Brill

Talk about the words you and your friends have chosen. Can you think of any better ones as you talk?

The neighbour's dog

Mrs Macy has just found out about the stray dog which Mr Macy keeps in the shed. She has ordered him to get rid of it at once.

He opened the shed door and out ambled a dog — a big, yellowy-white old dog, looking a bit like a sheep, somehow,
5   and about as quick-witted. As though it didn't notice what a tantrum Mrs Macy was in, it blundered gently towards her, and she lifted her broom high, and Mr Macy covered his eyes; and then Mrs Macy let out a real scream — a plain shriek — and dropped the broom and shot indoors and slammed the door after her.

The dog seemed puzzled, naturally; and so was I. It
10   lumbered around towards Mr Macy, and then I saw its head properly, and that it had the most extraordinary eyes — like headlamps, somehow. I don't mean as big as headlamps, of course, but with a kind of whitish glare to them. Then I realised that the poor old thing must be blind.

' 15   The dog had raised its nose inquiringly towards Mr Macy, and Mr Macy had taken one timid, hopeful step towards the dog, when one of the sash-windows of the house went up and Mrs Macy leaned out. She'd recovered from her panic, and she gave Mr Macy his orders. He was to take that disgusting
20   animal and turn it out into the road, where he must have found it in the first place.

I knew that old Macy would be too dead scared to do anything else but what his wife told him.

I went down again to where the others were having tea.
25   "Well?" said Mum.

I told them, and I told them what Mrs Macy was making Mr Macy do to the blind dog. "And if it's turned out like that on the road, it'll be killed by the first car that comes along."

What the Neighbours Did
Philippa Pearce

1 What was Mrs Macy going to do with the dog at first?
2 What was wrong with the dog?
3 What is Mr Macy told to do with the dog?
4 Where was the dog kept?
5 What did the boy think would happen to the dog?
6 In your own words say what the boy told his family.
7 What do you think the boy wanted to happen to the dog? What would you want to happen?
8 Write the words from the lists below which fit these people.

Mr Macy: brave   kind   helpful
            strong   hen-pecked
Mrs Macy: nice   nasty   excitable   bossy
            caring
The boy: observant   nosey   thoughtful
            worried   frightened

9 See if you can work out what these words in the passage mean.
    ambled (line 1)   tantrum (line 4)
    timid (line 16)   lumbered (line 10)
    blundered (line 4)   inquiringly (line 15)
   Look them up in a dictionary to check your answers.
10 Do you think the child was being a "nosey parker" watching what happened next door? Should people watch what their neighbours do? Give reasons for your answer.

Bottersnikes

Bottersnikes are the laziest creatures, probably, in the whole world.

They are too lazy to dig burrows, like rabbits, or to find hollow trees to live in as the small animals do, and would be
5 horrified at the work of building nests, like birds. Bottersnikes find their homes ready made, in rubbish heaps. When they find a pile of tins, pots, pans and junk, they think it is lovely, and crawl in. And live there, sleeping mostly. Best of all they like the rubbish heaps along dusty roadsides in the lonely
10 Australian bush, where they can sleep for weeks, undisturbed.

Once, in a rubbish heap like this, two long black ears poked out of a watering can. The ears came first because they were twice as long as the head they belonged to. Between the ears appeared an ugly green face with slanted eyes, a nose like a
15 cheese grater and a mean mouth with pointed teeth sticking out. The skin was wrinkly all over and little toadstools grew where the eyebrows should have been.

This was the King of the Bottersnikes. He squeezed out of the watering can.

20 ·The King's ears turned bright red because he was angry — this always happens with Bottersnikes when they get angry — and the cause of his temper was a thistle growing through the bottom of his bed. But he was too lazy to pull it out and just stood there looking, with his ears growing redder. Near him
25 he saw an old rusting car, propped against a gum tree. What a palace that would make for a Bottersnike King! "If someone would open the door," he thought, "I would get in."

So the King yelled at the top of his voice for help — and very loud that is; but the other Bottersnikes, all twenty or so of
30 the King's band, snored loudly from their beds in the rubbish to show they had not heard.

Bottersnikes and Gumbles
S. A. Wakefield

1 What kind of houses do Bottersnikes like best?
2 Why do Bottersnikes not build their own house?
3 How can you tell when Bottersnikes are angry?
4 Why did the King leave his watering can?
5 Why do Bottersnikes like the lonely Australian bush?
6 How many Bottersnikes were there?
7 What did the King of the Bottersnikes look like? Illustrate your answer.
8 Why did the Kings ears grow redder?
9 What do you think is the worst dream a Bottersnike could have?
10 How do we know that the King was unkind to the others?
11 Do you think these statements are true or false? Give reasons for your answers.

a Children like Bottersnikes as pets.
b Bottersnikes are the laziest creatures in the world.
c They go to great trouble to have an easy time.
d Bottersnikes eat a great deal.
e Bottersnikes' eyebrows are smooth and dark.
f They take great care of their teeth.

12 Make up an animal of your own. Describe what it is like and what it does. Draw a picture of it, if you like.

Barney and the cat

Barney moved from his house on a farm to a flat in a large town. His mother and father were out at work all day. He missed everything about the countryside, but most of all his pet rabbits.

The first thing Barney knew of the all-white cat was a scratchy noise. Barney thought it was a mouse and he sat mouse-still on his stool. Because it was such a rain-gloomy day he had left all the lights on — even the one in the tiny
5   entry hall. He could see it plainly as he leaned forwards, and his eyes got big with surprise because it wasn't a mouse, it was a white paw, white as any rabbit's. But it was a cat — there were claws.

A cat! Oh, if he could only have a cat in here with him.
10 Could he sneak to the door, jerk it open and grab the surprised cat before it could run? Aw, but a cat that could hear the slightest mouse sounds would hear him come, and run. Dang it, and he'd promised Mother up and down and sideways — she was so scared of this big town — that when he
15 was alone he'd never leave the apartment, not as much as one step.

Barney glanced around for something to lure the cat through the door into the apartment, saw a small piece of paper under the telephone and grabbed it. He poked in his
20 pocket for the piece of string that he kept just for knotting and unknotting. He crumpled the small sheet of paper and tied the string around one end so tight that the other end cupped and flared out like a skirt. If he danced the cupped paper along the crack under the door, then when the cat started to follow it,
25 he'd ease the door open and lead the cat inside with the

dancing, crackling paper. Then quickly shut the door, and he'd have a cat.

The Almost All-White Rabbity Cat
Meindert DeJong

1 What animal did Barney think made the scratching noise at first?
2 How did he know the animal was a cat and not a rabbit?
3 Where did he find the piece of paper?
4 What did the paper look like when he had tied the string round?
5 What sort of day was it outside?
6 What idea did Barney have for getting the cat into the room?
7 Describe all that Barney did with the paper and string.
8 Why didn't Barney go outside for the cat?
9 How do you think his mother would have felt if he had gone outside?
10 Why did he want the cat?
11 How was he feeling before the cat came?
12 Read the sentence in second paragraph that begins "Dang it . . ." What does this tell you about Barney, his mother and the place where they lived?

Catherine

The lines of this poem are mixed up. Read it and then answer the questions.

A She took some mud and mixed it up
   While adding water from a cup

B Catherine said "I think I'll bake
   A most delicious chocolate cake."

C And then she signed it "Fondly C."
   And gave the whole of it to me.

D And then some weeds and nuts and bark
   And special gravel from the park

E And on the top she wrote "To You"
   The way she says the bakers do

F I thanked her but I wouldn't dream
   Of eating cake without ice cream.

G A thistle and a dash of sand.
   She beat out all the lumps by hand.

Karla Kuskin

1 What was used in the making of the cake?
2 How did she get rid of the lumps?
3 Why did she write 'To You' on the top?
4 Who do you think Catherine is?
5 Discuss the order of the poem with your friends. Write out what you think is the correct order using the letters at the side. Are there other possible orders, or is yours the only one?

Chester's undoing

Here is a poem where the lines are not in the correct order.
Read it then answer the questions:

A A great long trail of crinkly wool
   Followed Chester down to school.

B Chester Lester Kirkenby Dale
   Caught his sweater on a nail.

C Chester undid from his head
   To his toes.

D Then his ears unravelled!
   His neck and his nose!

E Chester's undone, one un-purl, two unplain,
   Who's got the pattern to knit him again?

F As Chester started to travel
   So his sweater began to unravel.

Julie Holder

1 Read the poem again then write out the order as you
   think it should be, using the letters at the side of each pair
   of lines. Talk with your friends about your order. Give
   reasons for your choice.
2 How did Chester catch his sweater?
3 What stitches were in Chester's sweater?
4 Make up another title for this poem.

The loss of dark

A King and a crocodile played a game of chance. The loser had to give the winner any gift he asked.

The King lost and the crocodile asked for all the dark in his Kingdom.

5   King Merrion went home to his palace, where he found everyone in the greatest dismay and astonishment. For instead of there being night, as would have been proper at that time, the whole country was bathed in a strange unearthly light, clear as day, but a day in which nothing cast any
10   shadow. Flowers which had shut their petals opened them again, birds peevishly brought their heads out from under their wings, owls and bats, much puzzled, returned to their thickets, and the little princess Gurdrun refused to go to bed.

Indeed, after a few days, the unhappy King realized that he
15   had brought a dreadful trouble to his Kingdom — and to the whole world — by his rash promise. Without a regular spell of dark every twelve hours, nothing went right — plants grew tall and weak and spindly, cattle and poultry became confused and stopped producing milk and eggs, winds gave up
20   blowing, and the weather went all to pieces. As for people, they were soon in a worse muddle than the cows and hens. At first everybody tried to work all night, so as to make the most of this extra daylight, but they soon became cross and exhausted and longed for rest. However it was almost
25   impossible to sleep, for no matter what they did, covering their windows with thick curtains, shutting their doors, hiding under the bedclothes and bandaging their eyes, not a scrap of dark could anybody find. The crocodile had swallowed it all.

As for the children, they ran wild. Bed-time had ceased to
30   exist.

A Small Pinch of Weather
J. Aiken

1 What did the people try to do at first?
2 What did Gurdrun like more than anything else?
3 What did the loser of the game have to give the winner?
4 How did the people try to get to sleep?
5 What happened to the cows and hens?
6 In your own words describe what the King found when he first went home to his palace.
7 What effect did the continued daylight have on animals and plants?
8 The absence of dark affected children and adults in different ways. Write about what happened to each.
9 Do you think the children liked being without darkness?
10 Why were there no shadows?
11 What do you think is going to happen next in the story?
12 Explain in your own words what is meant by these phrases.

   a game of chance
   his rash promise
   went all to pieces
   such a state of affairs

13 Write words you could use instead of these from the passage

   dismay (line 6)   confused (line 18)
   ceased (line 29)   rash (line 16)
   bathed (line 8)   peevish (line 11)
   astonishment (line 6)

Calling on Biddy

Vernon and Jess went very slowly on towards the bare patch in front of the hut. Jess was so frightened that she found it hard to put one foot before the other, for now they knew Biddy was some kind of witch, and Biddy had warned her and
5 Frank to keep away. Vernon, Jess suspected, was almost as frightened as she was. It showed when he tried to make her go first between the petrol-drums, and it showed again when the cockerel flew up to the roof. Both of them ducked and put one arm up. Jess nearly ran away, only Vernon caught her coat
10 and would not let her go.

Biddy did not seem to be there. Jess hoped she was out — shopping, or something. She had often seen Biddy out shopping, with a string bag, all stooped over, peering through her glasses and taking big, irregular, swooping steps. Jess
15 prayed she was doing it now. Vernon fidgeted and seemed to get over being frightened.

"I think she's out," Jess whispered.

"Shall we see?" Vernon asked, with a sideways sort of grin at her. Before Jess could stop him, he picked up a stick and
20 hammered at a petrol drum with it.

A hen squawked. The cat darted out of another drum and ran crouching into the hut. She and Vernon stood in deep silence, until they heard a small shuffling inside the hut. Jess gasped. Vernon's eyes blinked whitely over at her. Then
25 Biddy Iremonger came ambling cheerfully out through the door, still wearing her sack.

"Yes?" she said merrily. "Somebody knocking for me?"

Wilkins' Tooth
D. Wynne Jones

40

1 Who is Biddy?
2 Where did Biddy live?
3 What did the children hear inside the hut?
4 What made Jess think that Vernon was frightened too?
5 How did Vernon stop Jess from running away?
6 What did the children do when they heard the shuffling noise?
7 What do you think made this shuffling noise?
8 How did Jess feel when she said "I think she's out"?
9 Some phrases tell you how Jess was feeling. One is "Jess nearly ran away." Write out all the others you can find.
10 Do you think the children were surprised by the way Biddy came to the door? What might they have expected?
11 Describe Biddy's hut as you imagine it to be.

Training Zero to beg

Jack and his uncle find a quiet place in the woods, where they begin to teach Jack's dog Zero to sit up and beg.

"Come on, then," Jack said. "Let's start the training. Here."

He handed up the bag of biscuits. He himself then crouched on all fours beside Zero, who was dozing.

5 "Hey, Zero!"

Zero opened his eyes and his ears pricked up slightly.

"Now — watch me!"

Zero yawned hugely and moved to a sitting position. He looked dazed.

10 "Now," whispered Jack to Uncle Parker, "you say 'UP!' and I'll sit up and beg. If I do it and he doesn't, you say, 'Good boy!' and pat my head, and give me the biscuit."

Uncle Parker nodded. He delved in the bag and came up with a chocolate digestive which he broke in half.

15 "Right."

He held the biscuit aloft half-way between Jack and Zero.

"Up. Sit up. Beg. Good boy — boys, rather."

Jack accordingly crouched on his legs and held his hands drooping forward in imitation of front paws.

20 "Good boy!" exclaimed Uncle Parker. He patted Jack on the head and held out the biscuit. Jack opened his mouth and Uncle Parker pushed the half digestive into it. It nearly choked him. He looked sideways to see that Zero was looking distinctly interested. For one thing, his eyes were fixed

25 soulfully on the piece of biscuit still protruding from Jack's mouth, and for another, he was doing a kind of stamping movement with his front paws alternately, like a race horse impatient to be loosed.

42

"Look!" The exclamation came out with a shower of crumbs. "Look at his paws!"

Uncle Parker nodded.

"We're on the right track. All we've got to do now is keep on reinforcing the message."

Absolute Zero
Helen Cresswell

1 Where did Uncle Parker hold the biscuit?
2 Why did the biscuit nearly choke Jack?
3 Would you call Zero a lively, active dog? Give reasons for your answer.
4 Write an account of Uncle Parker's actions in this training.
5 How did Zero behave when Jack received the biscuit?
6 Do you think they will succeed in training Zero to beg?
7 Write out the sentences below in the order Jack did them.

He sat up and begged.
He thought Zero was interested.
He crouched on all fours.
He spoke to Zero.
He nearly choked on the biscuit.
He spoke to Uncle Parker.

8 Which of these methods is Jack using to train Zero?
hunger   imitation   fear   curiosity
example   praise
9 Why is Jack doing this: for his pleasure or the dog's?
10 Do you think it is right that animals should be trained in tricks like this?
11 How is training like this different from training such animals as guide dogs, sheep dogs, or police dogs?
12 Suppose you had been hidden in the woods watching this. What would you have thought?

If you'd had a camera, which is the funniest picture you could have taken?

Oliver to the rescue

Three children, Miranda, Lincoln and Pinks, and their dog Oliver were waiting in a country house for their parents to arrive for Christmas. It rained and rained until the low ground flooded. Lincoln went out to look for help, but the bridge over the river collapsed and he was stuck on the other side.

Pinks stood silent. The bull terrier strained to escape from her grasp. The big bullet-headed dog whined and barked with his eyes fixed on Lincoln across the foaming water.

"Poor old Oliver, he doesn't want to leave either," Miranda
5   said. She bent to comfort him. As she did so the idea came to her. What was too great a risk for Pinks to take might be worth trying with their dog.

"Haven't you two gone yet?" Lincoln called impatiently across the water.

10   Miranda stood up. The others must agree because it was their only chance. Even if they hated her for suggesting the idea they had to try.

"I've fixed the washing-line to Oliver's collar," she shouted. "When I flash my torch, call him and he'll swim with it across
15   to you."

At her side Pinks stopped crying.

"Won't he be washed away and drowned?" she asked. "What will happen if the line catches on a rock and breaks?"

"Anything could happen," admitted Miranda. "Oliver may
20   be drowned but we must risk it. He's a wonderful swimmer and there's a good chance he'll get across."

Across the water Lincoln was silent. Miranda wondered if he had heard what they meant to do.

"All right," he said at last. "Let him try."

25   The bull terrier nuzzled Miranda's hand as she made sure the line was securely fastened. It seemed as if he understood

44

the importance of his mission. When Lincoln called he paused for a second with his haunches slipping on the bank, then plunged straight into the icy water.

Castaway Christmas
Margaret J. Baker

1 What has happened to Lincoln?
2 What does Miranda fix to the dog's collar?
3 What does the passage tell you about the water?
4 What was the signal for Lincoln to call out?
5 What dangers did the dog face?
6 What is Miranda's plan?
7 What had been too great a risk for Pinks to try?
8 How do you think Lincoln feels?
9 What did Lincoln want the girls to do?
10 How do you think Miranda feels as the dog swims across the water?
11 Does this happen during the day or night? Give reasons for your answer.
12 Below are five sentences which tell you what happened *before* this passage. Rewrite them in the correct order.

The girls found him at last and tried to throw a line.
The river burst its banks and broke the bridge.
Pinks wanted to swim over with the line.
The river rose further and was impossible for him to cross.
Lincoln was stranded in the dark on the far side.

13 Write a story about an escape from danger. Think of a clever way of escaping. Make it as exciting as you can.

The Flower Corner

This passage tells you about a row of shops between a market and a bus station. Read it to decide where everything is then answer the questions on the opposite page.

"The Flower Corner" was busy today because it was Thursday, and Thursday was one of the two market days held each week.

5   Mrs Holmes loved being busy as the time passed very quickly and she had so much to tell her family when she got home about who'd been in the shop and what they'd bought.

Hers was the second shop after the bus station, the first being a sweet shop and tobacconist. There were six in the block, but the end one nearest to the market had been empty

10 since Woolworths had moved into the shopping precinct round the corner

She had thought of moving herself, but she'd noticed that people often called for flowers on their way back from the market when their bags were heavy and their arms full.

15 Perhaps if she'd moved they wouldn't have been as tempted to buy flowers, since they would have had to carry them so much further. At least, that was what Mr Greenwood, the manager of the shoe shop next door to hers thought.

Mrs Holmes opened early and brought out the green metal

20 vases filled with fresh water ready to receive the supply of fresh flowers which Dennis Matthews, the greengrocer, whose shop was next to the empty Woolworths shop, would bring. He had a waggon and went very early three times a week to get fresh supplies from the Wholesale Market. Mrs Holmes

25 and he shared the cost of the petrol so they both benefited from the arrangement.

Usually he was back by now, about 8.30 a.m., which just gave her time to collect her boxes of flowers, put them into water before doing some shopping for herself at the supermarket next to the shoe shop.

1 Why did Mrs Holmes not move from the "Flower Corner"?
2 Which firm had been in the end shop? Why was it empty now?
3 Why did Dennis Matthews bring Mrs Holmes flowers?
4 What time of the day is this taking place?
5 Which shops were on each side of the supermarket?
6 Who were Mr Greenwood's neighbours?

Make a sketch to show all the information about this row of shops.

First published 1982
Reprinted 1982, 1983, 1985

Basil Blackwell Limited
108 Cowley Road
Oxford
OX4 1JF

ISBN 0 631 91550 8

Acknowledgements

We are grateful to the following for permission to reproduce copyright material:
Harper and Row, Publishers, Inc. for "Catherine" from *In the Middle of the Trees* by Karla Kuskin; the author for "Chester's Undoing" by Julie Holder from *A Second Poetry Book* published by Oxford University Press.

Typesetting by Getset (BTS) Ltd, Eynsham Oxford

Printed in Great Britain